THE PRINCIPLE OF ONENESS

A Practical Guide to Experiencing the Profound Unity of Everything

"You are not a drop in the ocean.
You are the entire ocean,
in a drop."
—Rumi

RUSSELL ANTHONY GIBBS

Copyright © 2017 Russell Anthony Gibbs.

All Rights Reserved. No part(s) of this book may be reproduced, distributed or transmitted in any form, or by any means, or stored in a database or retrieval systems without prior expressed written permission of the author of this book.

ISBNs:
978-1-5356-0788-9 (paperback)
978-1-5356-0789-6 (hardback)

Contents

Introduction 1
Important Definitions 7

The Principle of Oneness 15
1. Defining the Principle of Oneness 15
   A. The Universe is 95 Percent Unknown 22
   B. Everything is an Infinite Field of Energy 24
   C. This Field of Energy is Identified as The Universe/
      God 25
   D. All Energy and Matter is Identical at
      its Subatomic Core 28
   E. Everything has a Degree of Consciousness 29
   F. The Collective Consciousness Controls and
      Manifests Everything 31
   G. The Universe/God Energy Field Transcends
      Space and Time 34
   H. The Universe/God Energy Field is in a Constant
      State of Change 36
   Summary of the Principle of Oneness 39

2. The Key Aspects of God/The Universe 41
   A. There are Many Misconceptions Regarding God/
      The Universe 41
   B. God/The Universe is Within Us 44
   C. God/The Universe is a Democracy of One 47
   Summary of the Key Aspects of God/The Universe 48

3. Living the Principle of Oneness 51
   1. Know the Magnitude of Who and What You Are ... 52
      A. See Yourself in Everything and Everyone 53
      B. Transcend the Limits of the Personal Ego 59
      C. Realize you are Eternal and Transcend Space and Time. 61
      D. Seek All Answers and all Change from Within .. 63
   2. Choose to Love Every Facet of Yourself Unconditionally. 66
      A. Love Yourself (Your Personal Consciousness) Unconditionally. 66
      B. Love Your Broader Self (Other People) Unconditionally. 68
      C. Love the Nonhuman Aspects of the Universe/God. 72
      D. Love God/The Universe. 75
      E. Identify and Transcend all Negative Feelings 76
   Summary Of Living The Principle Of Oneness 78

Conclusion 79
Special Message to the Reader 81
About the Author 83
Acknowledgments 85
Index of Quoted Authors and Sacred Texts 87
Sacred Text References 87
Quoted Authors 89

Introduction

The Principle of Oneness is the second book in a series of eight books on enlightenment. The first book, ***The Six Principles of Enlightenment and Meaning of Life***, is an intellectual and spiritual overview of enlightenment principles that explain the nature of our existence. This book, ***The Principle of Oneness***, expands on the first principle and clarifies the universe's profound interconnectedness. I am referencing several sacred texts, and I have again incorporated quotes from enlightened beings, scientists, spiritual leaders, artists, philosophers and others to support the explanations. I purposely repeat some particularly important and profound quotes to reinforce the messages. If you are unfamiliar with any of the quoted authors in this book, please reference the Index of Quoted Authors and Sacred Texts in the back. Additionally, I have provided practical methods to live and experience the Principle of Oneness. This book is intended to be a stand-alone work; the other five principles from the first book are referenced when necessary, to illuminate the Principle of Oneness.

These are the six principles of enlightenment:

The Principle of Oneness
The Principle of Manifestation
The Principle of Multiple Realities
The Principle of Timelessness
The Principle of Neutrality and Nonjudgement
The Principle of Openness

If you intellectually understand and emotionally experience the Principle of Oneness, you can achieve enlightenment. Science and certain philosophies, such as Buddhism, tend to offer an intellectual, logical approach to explain the Principle of Oneness. Christianity and certain other religions often offer an emotional, faith-based approach. Both approaches are worthy means to help comprehend the Principle of Oneness, and your path should be guided by your personal preference for understanding.

Enlightenment is not an exclusive club for a chosen few intellectuals or spiritual elites. Some of the quoted authors in this book are not well-known and include actors, poets, entertainers, travel writers, politicians, fiction writers and even comedians. These authors' profound quotes are a clear indication that many more people have had glimpses of enlightenment and have lived wisely, than we may realize.

Enlightened beings often live among us with little fame or notoriety further demonstrating that enlightenment is available to everyone.

Why Seek Enlightenment?

Enlightenment can be defined as a profound, intellectual and spiritual awakening to your higher consciousness. Enlightenment can also be one's self-realization that leads to the end of suffering and a state of bliss, or in Buddhist terms, nirvana. Confusion, suffering, pain and faltering through life is the opposite approach to enlightened living. While enlightenment is not necessary to exist, it makes your journey in life much less difficult and far more enjoyable.

Furthermore, Deepak Chopra identifies two signs (or symptoms) of enlightenment from Vedanta, one of the six orthodox schools of Indian philosophy. Having these two symptoms of enlightenment could also make life significantly more enjoyable and meaningful.

> According to Vedanta,
> there are only two symptoms of enlightenment,
> just two indications that a transformation
> is taking place within you toward a higher consciousness.
> The first symptom is that you stop worrying.
> Things don't bother you anymore.
> You become light-hearted and full of joy.
> The second symptom is that you encounter more
> and more meaningful coincidences in your life,
> more and more synchronicities.
> And this accelerates to the point where you actually
> experience the miraculous.
> —Deepak Chopra

It is important in anyone's pursuit of enlightenment to discern for himself or herself whether something resonates with truth. In this book I'm referencing both ancient and contemporary wisdom. Much of enlightenment wisdom has been available for thousands of years but at times has been lost and/or misinterpreted. I'm purposely trying to connect the dots of science, religion and philosophy to give a unified explanation of the Principle of Oneness. Ultimately you must still trust your own reason and have the resolve to discern the truth of this principle.

Enlightenment is man's release
from his self-incurred tutelage.
Tutelage is man's inability to make use
of his understanding without direction from another.
Self-incurred is this tutelage when its cause lies
not in lack of reason but in lack of resolution
and courage to use it without direction from another.
Sapere aude! "Have courage to use your own reason!"
—that is the motto of enlightenment.
—Immanuel Kant

"I shall no longer be instructed by the Yoga Veda
or the Aharva Veda, or the ascetics,
or any other doctrine whatsoever.
I shall learn from myself, be a pupil of myself;
I shall get to know myself, the mystery of Siddhartha."
He looked around as if he were seeing the world
for the first time.
—Hermann Hesse

Enlightenment means
taking full responsibility for your life.
—William Blake

Important Definitions

There are several terms and concepts used in this book that are worth clarifying at the beginning. Here is a short list of some key terms and concepts used to explain the Principle of Oneness.

Quantum Mechanics

Also referred to as quantum physics or quantum field theory, quantum mechanics is a branch of study that explains the behavior of matter and energy on the molecular, atomic and subatomic levels. Quantum mechanics deals with the laws governing the very small pieces of matter and energy that make up everything in the universe. The universe is a quantum field of energy and matter. This quantum field is constantly transforming from energy to matter, then back to energy again. When matter is broken down or energy is collided, the other is created. This cycle is fundamental to understanding ourselves and our reality.

The more you understand the theories of quantum mechanics, the stranger they seem. On the atomic and subatomic levels, matter and energy behave entirely differently from what we see on a bigger scale in the physical world. On a large scale, the world appears as a variety of objects that can be solid, liquid or gas. On an atomic level, there appears to be nothing solid and 99.99 percent empty space (atomic emptiness); the remainder is moving quickly and phasing in and out, with no exact position in space. On an atomic level, everything is moving in a constant state of flux with indeterminate positions. Again, none of this matches up with the solid, stable, physical world we perceive and experience in our ordinary reality.

String Theories

Superstring theories (*string theories* for short) explain that what we thought were single, point-like particles—such as an electron, proton or neutron—are actually small string-like, vibrating filaments. String theories began in the late 1960s and continue to be postulated today. M-Theory is a theory that unifies all consistent versions of superstring theory. Because string theories try to incorporate all the fundamental interactions of the universe, including gravity, many physicists hope that it will be the theory of everything. String theory also proposes that all the strings are identical and the properties of a particle—like its mass and charge—are determined by the vibrational state of the string. Therefore all energy and matter at its core is identical, and only its vibrational frequency gives it its unique characteristics.

Consciousness

The concept of consciousness has perplexed both philosophers and scientists alike for centuries. Consciousness can be defined as a state or quality of awareness. It could also be described as the source of all cognitive processes, from which thoughts, beliefs and emotions originate. There are various theories about where consciousness is located. Some scientists and philosophers believe consciousness (or the mind) is nonphysical and separate of the physical being (dualism), while others think it could be contained in the brain as a neural activity (materialism). Earlier philosophers such as Plato and Aristotle connected consciousness to the concept of the soul or spirit and were dualist in their thinking.

One additional view about consciousness, known as panpsychism, is that everything material—even down to the subatomic level—has individual consciousness. This means *everything* has a degree or type of consciousness, including plants, dirt, air, water and even man-made structures. Panpsychism is one of the oldest philosophical theories about consciousness and can be found in the teachings of Vedanta, Mahayana Buddhism, Shinto, Taoism, Paganism, Shamanism, Plato, Aristotle, Baruch Spinoza and Charles Darwin. I ascribe to the concept of panpsychism and believe that a shared consciousness is the conduit that unifies the Universe.

The renowned psychologist Carl Jung and neurologist Sigmund Freud further theorized that consciousness has at least three different layers of awareness. Although their layers differ in name and type, they add a complexity and depth to consciousness. Both Jung and Freud believed that most of our consciousness is not easily accessible and that the small part that was can be compared with the tip of an iceberg. Jung's deepest layer of consciousness, the collective unconscious, is the layer shared by beings of the same species. I believe that there are possibly many more than three layers to consciousness and that on the deepest layer there is shared consciousness of the entire Universe—not only humans but animals, plants and anything material down to a subatomic level. There could be personal and group consciousness based upon gender, nationality, ethnicity or anything a person chooses to identify with. Then there are several layers of less accessible subconsciousness—both personal and group—and additional layers of unconsciousness that are personal, group and collective. All these layers of connected consciousness add to the complexity of the cognitive processes of the entire Universe.

Emotions

Emotions are complex and can be described as instinctive states or intuitive feelings derived from one's circumstances. Scientists have not come to a consensus on what actually triggers emotions or their function. There are three types of theories that emotions, however, could be triggered physiologically, neurologically or cognitively. That is, emotions could be triggered by your physical body, your brain activities or your thought processes.

I believe that emotions could be triggered by all three but are primarily a product of our cognitive processes. Among other things, emotions tell us how we are thinking. They are signals of consistency or conflict with our thoughts and beliefs in different layers of consciousness. Positive emotions feel good and signal consistent thoughts and beliefs in the conscious, subconscious and unconscious layers. Negative emotions feel unpleasant and signal conflicting thoughts and beliefs in the various layers of consciousness. Emotions are efficient signals of our thoughts and beliefs, and are a shortcut to doing deep analysis of our cognitive process. I believe that the broader consciousness as a whole sends itself emotions as indications of the general state of being. Emotions reveal whether the thoughts in our personal consciousness are consistent and in agreement with the collective consciousness.

The Universe/God

The Universe, or God, describes the infinite entity that encompasses "all that is." The Universe/God is known by many names, including the Divine, Allah, the Great Spirit, Mother Nature, the Force and the soul. Much is unknown or misinterpreted regarding the nature of the Universe/God, and there has been some speculation that the human mind may not be capable of comprehending the enormity of the concept. Regardless of our human mental capacity, we are by definition part of "all that is" and consequently part of the Universe/God.

Anthropomorphism

Anthropomorphism is the attribution of human qualities, emotions, motivations or physical form to non-human entities, such as inanimate objects, animals or a deity. In mythology and religion there is a rich history of many deities in human form acting with love, aggression and even vengeance.

Pantheism

Pantheism is the belief that the universe and nature in its totality, is the Divine and that God is an impersonal entity. Pantheists may also view the entire universe as a manifestation of God. Consequentially, pantheists tolerate the worship of all gods of different faiths, cultures or societies without prejudice.

The Principle of Oneness

1. Defining the Principle of Oneness

The Principle of Oneness explains that everything in the universe both seen and unseen is connected and part of one entity. Throughout history this entity has been identified as the Universe, God, the Soul, the Great Spirit, the Divine, Allah, Brahma the Creator, Jehovah, Mother Nature and countless other names. This entity, the Universe/God, is "all that is" and includes "nothingness." The Universe/God appears as infinite individual expressions of consciousness, energy and other matter, similar to cells within a body. We are all like cells within the body of the Universe/ God—as are plants, animals, air, natural resources and everything down to a subatomic level. Like cells in a body, these expressions grow, create, divide, destroy, die and are reabsorbed into the Universe/God to create again. From the perspective of quantum mechanics, the Universe is an infinite quantum field of tiny pieces of energy and matter that convert back and forth. On a subatomic level all this energy and matter is identical at its core. Because all this energy is identical, it cannot be determined where anything begins or ends on the subatomic level. Nothing in the Universe/God is ever lost or gained but simply a field of energy and matter in a constant state of flux. We are all part of one big energy organism expressing and experiencing itself.

Again, we and everything seen and unseen are contained within this field of energy and matter. Matter has mass and is comprised of atoms composed of particles of protons, neutrons and electrons. Energy is more abstract and does not have mass but can move or elicit change in matter. Light, heat, sound, gravity, electromagnetic fields and nuclear fission and fusion are all forms of energy. When religion, philosophy and literature discuss this energy field, light is frequently the symbolic form of energy referenced. Light is also the root word of enlightenment. Light energy often symbolizes knowledge, wisdom, healing, goodness, love, the Universe/God and Oneness.

> Again Jesus spoke to them, saying,
> "I am the light of the world.
> Whoever follows me will never walk in darkness
> but will have the light of life."
> —John 8:12 (NRSV)

> The Warrior of the Light is a believer.
> Because he believes in miracles, miracles begin to happen.
> Because he is sure that his thoughts can change his life,
> his life begins to change.
> Because he is certain that he will find love,
> love appears.
> —Paulo Coelho

> We can easily forgive a child who is afraid of the dark;
> the real tragedy of life
> is when men are afraid of the light.
> —Plato

> You have to find what sparks a light in you
> so that you in your own way can illuminate the world.
> —Oprah Winfrey

> The wound is the place where the Light enters you.
> —Rumi

Our connections to the Oneness of the Universe/God are both physical/atomic matter and nonphysical spiritual/energy. What we can see and measure we consider physical reality, composed of atomic matter. What we cannot always see but can experience or measure the effects of, we consider nonphysical, spiritual reality, composed of energy.

Here are several examples to further illustrate physical matter versus nonphysical energy:

Physical/Atomic Matter	Nonphysical/Energy
Brain	Consciousness
Neural/synaptic activity	Thoughts, beliefs and emotions
Physical reality	Heaven, hell or the afterlife
Physical body	Soul/spirit
Man	God

According to quantum mechanics, everything is either matter or energy and nothing exists outside this. Energy and matter cannot be created or destroyed but only converted from one form to another. $E=mc^2$ is Albert Einstein's special theory of relativity equation that postulates that energy is equal to mass times the speed of light squared. Energy and matter are like two different sides of the same coin: when you break down matter (an atom), you release a huge amount of energy, known as a nuclear reaction. When you smash or collide two or more forms of energy (photons), you actually create matter. In this field, energy and matter are constantly converting back and forth from one to the other, or so it seems. Einstein drew a startling conclusion regarding matter and energy.

> Concerning matter, we have been all wrong.
> What we have called matter is energy,
> whose vibration has been so lowered
> as to be perceptible to the senses.
> There is no matter.
> —Albert Einstein

According to Einstein, only energy exists and physical matter is merely slower moving (lower vibrating) energy. All energy and matter on a subatomic level is vibrating but at different speeds, and that gives everything its unique characteristics. The faster energy moves/vibrates, the harder it is to observe with our senses. The energy still exists, but we can see it only if we can raise our vibrational perceptions (consciousness) to detect it. A visual metaphor for this concept is a hummingbird's wings. A typical hummingbird moves very quickly, flapping its wing fifty times per second. When viewed by the human eye, the wings are moving so quickly they virtually disappear. If you could raise your visual perceptions to match the speed of the wings, like that of a high-speed camera, you could then perceive the wings. Like the humming bird's wings, faster vibrating energy is not always visible to the human senses, but it does nevertheless exist.

So if Einstein was correct and there is no matter, the physical reality we live in is just an intricate illusion of slow-moving energy. This is plausible because on a subatomic level, 99.999 percent of what we believe is physical matter; is in fact empty space. This vast atomic emptiness between a nucleus of an atom and an electrons orbiting has been compared with the distance of a planet orbiting a sun, with nothing in between. Based upon quantum mechanics, our physical reality should not be solid. Most likely our physical reality is an elaborate illusion within our own consciousness and the collective consciousness of the Universe/God. The illusion of physical world is a product of the underlying energy field, the Universe/God. That is why God, in his many names, has been identified as the creator of everything. Although this is theoretically correct, it doesn't explain that everything already existed in the energy field but did not become physical and visible until the vibration was slowed. The physical world as an elaborate illusion has been referenced in science, religion and philosophy for thousands of years. The only true reality may be the underlying energy field identified as the soul/the Universe/God.

> Reality is merely an illusion,
> albeit a very persistent one.
> —Albert Einstein

> The first principles of the universe
> are atoms and empty space;
> everything else is merely thought to exist.
> —Democritus

Matter, that thing the most solid and the well-known,
which you are holding in your hands
and which makes up your body,
is now known to be mostly empty space.
Empty space and points of light.
What does this say about the reality of the world?
—Jeanette Winterson

What you are seeing and hearing right now
is nothing but a dream.
You are dreaming right now in this moment.
You are dreaming with the brain awake.
—Don Miguel Ruiz

Suffering just means you're having a bad dream.
Happiness means you're having a good dream.
Enlightenment means getting out of the dream altogether.
—Jed McKenna

Do not be misled by what you see around you,
or be influenced by what you see.
You live in a world which is a playground of illusion,
full of false paths, false values and false ideals.
But you are not part of that world.
—Sai Baba

We live in illusion and the appearance of things.
There is a reality. We are that reality.
When you understand this, you see that you are nothing,
and being nothing, you are everything.
That is all.
—Kalu Rinpoche

> God had brought me to my knees
> and made me acknowledge my own nothingness,
> and out of that knowledge I had been reborn.
> I was no longer the centre of my life
> and therefore I could see God in everything.
> —Bede Griffiths

> I am not this hair, I am not this skin,
> I am the soul that lives within.
> —Rumi

When explaining the Principle of Oneness, it is helpful to break down the explanation into a list of key interrelated aspects. Here are the fundamental aspects regarding the Principle of Oneness with supporting quotes from various authors.

A. The Universe Is 95 Percent Unknown

The universe is not what it appears to be, and we have only a basic understanding of less than 5 percent of it. In 2001, the Wilkinson Microwave Anisotropy Probe (or WMAP) helped NASA to map out the composition of the visible universe. According to NASA we can only identify 4.6 percent of the visible universe as physical, baryonic matter made of atoms, composed of protons, neutrons and electrons. The remaining 95 percent of the observable universe is unknown substances that cannot be seen or measured but are identified as dark matter (24 percent) and dark energy (71 percent). Dark matter and dark energy are believed to exist because we can measure gravitational distortions and extrapolate their percentages. In addition, the 4.6 percent of the universe that we believe is solid matter, on a sub-atomic level is 99.999 percent empty space (atomic emptiness). Our physical reality is most likely an elaborate illusion within our consciousness and the collective consciousness. Consequently, we do not truly know and understand the universe, ourselves or the nature of our reality.

> If quantum mechanics hasn't profoundly shocked you,
> you haven't understood it yet.
> Everything we call real
> is made of things that cannot be regarded as real.
> —Niels Bohr

> By faith we understand that the worlds were prepared
> by the word of God, so that what is seen
> was made from things that are not visible.
> —Hebrews 11:3 (NRSV)

> The day science begins to study non-physical phenomena,
> it will make more progress in one decade
> than in all the previous centuries of its existence.
> —Nikola Tesla

B. Everything Is an Infinite Field of Energy

Everything on a subatomic level in the physical and nonphysical universe is part of one infinite field of energy/matter swirling, moving and vibrating at various speeds. All our energies are comingled, like water in the ocean. On a subatomic level, it is not possible to determine where anything begins or ends, because there is no true separation of individual energy despite the illusions of the physical realities. Nothing exists outside this field of energy and matter. The essence of our Oneness is our connection to this infinite field of energy and matter.

> One drop of the sea cannot claim to come from one river,
> and another drop of the sea from another river;
> the sea is a single consistent whole.
> In the same way all beings are one;
> there is no being that does not come from the soul,
> and is not part of the soul.
> —The Chandogya Upanishad

> We are all connected.
> To each other, biologically.
> To the earth, chemically.
> To the rest of the universe, atomically.
> —Neil deGrasse Tyson

> Taoist philosophy is essentially monistic.
> Matter and energy, Yang and Yin, heaven and earth,
> are conceived of as essentially one
> or as two coexistent poles
> of one indivisible whole.
> —Bruce Lee

> In nature, action and reaction are continuous.
> Everything is connected to everything else.
> No one part, nothing, is isolated.
> Everything is linked, and interdependent.
> Everywhere everything is connected to everything else.
> Each question receives the correct answer.
> —Svami Prajnanpad

> Energy functioning in a pattern becomes matter.
> That is all life is ... Matter and energy are interrelated.
> —Jiddu Krishnamurti

C. This Field of Energy Is Identified as the Universe/God

This infinite field of energy over the course of history has been identified as the Universe, God, the Divine, the Soul, Allah, the Great Spirit, Mother Nature, the Force and many other names. This is important because it helps to unify a variety of religious, philosophical and pagan beliefs that often have an incomplete or misinterpretation of the concept of the Universe/God. Furthermore, this energy field, the Universe/God, is in us and we are in It. We are both part of the Universe/God and at the same time all of the Universe/God is contained within ourselves. This is an enormous concept to comprehend. It seems plausible that we are part the Universe/God. However, the concept that all of the Universe/God is contained within us is more challenging to comprehend. Several religions make reference to seeing the Divine in everything, but they often don't explain the complexity of this concept.

> He is fire and the sun; He is the moon and the stars;
> He is the air and the sea. He is this boy, and that girl.
> He appears in countless different forms.
> He has no beginning, and He has no end.
> He is the source of all things.
> Each type of living being is distinct and different.
> But when we pierce the veil of difference,
> we see the unity of all beings.
> —The Svetasvatara Upanishad

> Your greatest awakening comes,
> when you are aware about your infinite nature.
> —Amit Ray

The little space within the heart is as great
as the vast universe. The heavens and the earth are there,
and the sun and the moon and the stars.
Fire and lightening and winds are there,
and all that now is and all that is not.
—The Chandogya Upanishad

Though the eye is small, the soul which sees through it
is greater and vaster than all the things which it perceives.
In fact, it is so great that it includes all objects,
however large or numerous, within itself.
For it is not so much that you are within the cosmos
as that the cosmos is within you.
—Meher Baba

The cosmos is within us. We are made of star-stuff.
We are a way for the universe to know itself.
—Carl Sagan

We are not human beings having a spiritual experience.
We are spiritual beings having a human experience.
—Pierre Teilhard de Chardin

The Creator Himself, at one and the same time,
knowledge, the knower, and the known …
There exists nothing which is not united to Him
and which He does not find His own essence.
He is the type of all being, and all things exist in Him
under their most pure and most perfect form.
—Moses ben Jacob Cordovero

> When I do not know who I am, I serve you.
> When I know who I am, I am you.
> —Indian proverb

D. All Energy and Matter Is Identical at Its Subatomic Core

All energy and matter is identical at its subatomic core and appears different only because of the variations of speed or vibration. According to string theory in quantum mechanics the core of energy and matter on a subatomic level is a vibrating, string-like filament that is identical in all energy and matter. This is a startling revelation because when we look out into the physical world, we perceive a variety of things that we believe are both different and unique. One way to visualize this concept is to compare the various forms water can take: it can be liquid, ice, snow, hail, clouds, fog or invisible gaseous vapors. Ice can also be manipulated and sculpted creating various shapes and figures. Other forms of energy such as heat, can change the vibrational speed of the water and thus change its appearance from ice to liquid or liquid to gas. Regardless of the form, all of this is still water at its core. If everything that exists is identical at its subatomic core (identical vibrating strings), there is only one substance/energy in the Universe, which by definition is Oneness.

If you want to find the secrets of the universe,
think in terms of energy, frequency and vibration.
—Nikola Tesla

With even more precise observation,
the theory (string theory) argues,
you'd notice that the strings within different kinds of particles
are identical, the leitmotif of string unification,
but vibrate in different patterns.
—Brian Greene

Even when tied in a thousand knots,
the string is still but one.
—Rumi

Brahman is the clay of substance out of which
an infinite variety of articles are fashioned.
As clay, they are all one,
but form or manifestation differentiates them.
Before one of them was made,
they all existed potentially in clay,
and, of course, they are identical substantially;
but when formed, and so long as the form remains,
they are separate and different;
—Swami Vivekananda

E. Everything Has a Degree of Consciousness

Everything has a degree of consciousness and it is connected to a collective consciousness of the Universe/God. Consciousness can be defined as a state or quality of awareness. It can also be described as the source of all cognitive processes, where thoughts, beliefs and emotions originate. Consciousness is without mass and by deduction is a form of the energy that is connected to the energy field of the Universe/God. It is generally accepted that human and animals have degrees of consciousness, but this also means that even things we believe are inanimate; have a degree of consciousness. Many inanimate objects however, may not necessarily be self-conscious or self-aware. Nevertheless, consciousness exists in things such as plants, dirt, air, water and even man-made structures. This view regarding consciousness, known as panpsychism, is that everything material—even down to the subatomic level—has individual consciousness. This is one of the oldest philosophical theories about consciousness and can be found in the teachings of Vedanta, Mahayana Buddhism, Shinto, Taoism, Paganism, Shamanism, Plato, Aristotle, Baruch Spinoza and Charles Darwin. The shared collective consciousness of the Universe/God is the unifying thread in the Principle of Oneness.

> What is the soul? The soul is consciousness.
> It shines as the light within the heart.
> —The Brihadaranyaka Upanishad

> The energy of the mind is the essence of life.
> —Aristotle

> Consciousness is not in the body;
> the body is In Consciousness.
> —Dan Millman

> We are the cosmos made conscious,
> —and life is the means by which
> the universe understands itself.
> —Brian Cox

F. The Collective Consciousness Controls and Manifests Everything

The collective consciousness of the Universe/God is the control center of the physical world illusion and everyone/everything in it. Consciousness both personal and the collective can and does regulate, manipulate and control the vibrational frequencies of energy that forms our physical reality. The collective consciousness and all its branches of personal consciousness, through beliefs and thoughts, collide or smash energy, slowing down its vibration to create what we see as the physical world.

Our physical reality has no more material substance than a typical belief, thought or dream. It is merely slower vibrating energy. So the source of the physical world is the collective consciousness energy field that is also identified as the Universe/God and at times the soul. As part of the collective consciousness, our personal consciousness shares in the creation of our physical reality illusion. It is important to understand that all of us are all either consciously or unconsciously co-creating the illusions of the physical reality. We often are unaware of our co-creating ability and frequently create parts of the physical reality by default unconsciously. Through our thoughts and beliefs, we have created ourselves, others around us and our entire physical world. This process of creating is the **Principle of Manifestation** as explained in *The Six Principles of Enlightenment and Meaning of Life*.

It is worth repeating this important scientific quote from Albert Einstein about the illusion of physical matter, along with these other supporting quotes.

> Concerning matter, we have been all wrong.
> What we have called matter is energy,
> whose vibration has been so lowered
> as to be perceptible to the senses.
> There is no matter.
> —Albert Einstein

Energy is liberated matter,
matter is energy waiting to happen.
—Bill Bryson

Control of consciousness determines the quality of life.
—Mihaly Csikszentmihalyi

Today a young man on acid realized that all matter
is merely energy condensed to a slow vibration,
that we are all one consciousness experiencing itself subjectively,
there is no such thing as death, life is only a dream,
and we are the imagination of ourselves.
Here's Tom with the weather.
—Bill Hicks

The closer you come to knowing that you alone
create the world of your experience, the more vital it becomes
for you to discover just who is doing the creating.
—Eric Micha'el Leventhal

A fundamental conclusion of the new physics
also acknowledges that the observer creates the reality.
As observers, we are personally involved
with the creation of our own reality.
Physicists are being forced to admit that the universe
is a 'mental' construction.
—Richard Conn Henry

The stream of knowledge is heading toward
a non-mechanical reality;
the universe begins to look more like a great thought
than like a great machine.
Mind no longer appears to be an accidental intruder
into the realm of matter; we ought to hail it
as the creator and governor of the realm of matter.
Get over it, and accept the inarguable conclusion.
The universe is immaterial-mental and spiritual.
—Sir James Jeans

The universe is the energy of the soul;
and from this energy comes life,
consciousness, and the elements.
The universe is the will of the soul;
and from this will comes the law of cause and effect.
From the soul one become many;
but in the soul many are one.
—The Mundaka Upanishad

He is one, the Lord and innermost Self of all;
of one form, he makes of himself many forms.
To him who sees the Self revealed in his own heart
belongs eternal bliss.
—The Katha Upanishad

G. The Universe/God Energy Field Transcends Space and Time

The Universe/God energy field transcends both space and time and exists in infinite realities and infinite times. Both space and time are illusions created when parts of the energy field vibrates slow enough to be perceived by our senses. In the physical reality, there is the illusion of linear time resulting in the illusion of various time periods. There is also the illusion of physical space resulting in the illusion of multiple physical and nonphysical realities. These concepts, the **Principle of Multiply Realities** and the **Principle of Timelessness** are explained in the book *The Six Principles of Enlightenment and Meaning of Life*. We are one multidimensional being and exist in multiple universes transcending space and time. We could also be described as multiple personalities of the Universe/God. This is important because enlightenment involves comprehending the complexity of our Oneness and realizing our multidimensional existence. We are everything, everywhere at every time.

Einstein comes along and says,
space and time can warp and curve,
that's what gravity is.
Now string theory comes along and says,
yes, gravity, quantum mechanics, electromagnetism
—all together in one package, but only if the universe
has more dimensions than the ones that we see.
— Brian Greene

String theory envisions a multiverse in which our universe
is one slice of bread in a big cosmic loaf.
The other slices would be displaced from ours
in some extra dimension of space.
—Brian Greene

The universe bursts into existence from life,
not the other way around as we have been taught.
For each life there is a universe, its own universe.
We generate spheres of reality, individual bubbles of existence.
Our planet is comprised of billions of spheres of reality,
generated by each individual human
and perhaps even by each animal.
—Robert Lanza

The only reason for time
is so that everything doesn't happen at once.
—Albert Einstein

What we call "time" isn't chronological but spatial;
what we call "death" is merely a transition
between different kinds of matter.
—Stéphane Audeguy

> The Hopi, an Indian tribe, have a language
> as sophisticated as ours,
> but no tenses for past, present and future.
> The division does not exist.
> What does this say about time?
> —Jeanette Winterson

H. The Universe/God Energy Field Is in a Constant State of Change

The Universe/God energy field is in a constant state of change cycling from creation to destruction or birth to death. The Universe/God fluctuates from the appearance of many facets and then to Oneness then reverts back again to many facets. This is played out with the cycle of birth, death and reincarnation. This cycle of reincarnation is a fundamental pattern of our physical existence. Despite our appearance as many, we are all still one organism and long to be consolidated as one. We also long to expand and venture out; experiencing what appears to be separateness or individuality. The collective consciousness of the Universe/God longs to express itself in every possible variation in infinite realities transcending space and time. Then, because all energy and matter is identical at its core, it has a propensity to be drawn back to itself and reunite. This reunion is often the death of the physical form and the return to spiritual energy.

The energy in the world flows
from God at the center, and back to God.
The sages see life as a wheel, with each individual
going round and round and round through birth and death.
Individuals remain on this wheel
so long as they believe themselves to be separate;
but once they realize their unity with God,
then they break free.
—The Svetasvatara Upanishad

In this world there are two orders of being,
the perishable and the imperishable.
The perishable is all that is visible.
The imperishable is the invisible substance
of all that is visible.
—The Bhagavad Gita

Don't grieve.
Anything you lose comes round in another form.
—Rumi

I died as a mineral and became a plant,
I died as a plant and rose to animal,
I died as an animal and I was Man.
Why should I fear?
When was I less by dying?
—Rumi

Everything is connected, like a delicate web.
Ever growing, ever changing. New silvery strands
come together every day, and once the strand is formed,
no matter what superficial circumstances
may sometimes keep you apart, it is never broken.
You will meet again, perhaps in another lifetime.
The connection is unbreakable,
lying dormant in your subconscious.
—Chelsie Shakespeare

I am in exact accord with the belief of Thomas Edison
that spirit is immortal, that there is a continuing center
of character in each personality.
But I don't know what spirit is, nor matter either.
I suspect they are forms of the same thing.
I never could see anything in this reputed antagonism
between spirit and matter. To me this is the most beautiful,
the most satisfactory from a scientific standpoint,
the most logical theory of life.
For thirty years I have leaned toward
the theory of Reincarnation.
It seems a most reasonable philosophy
and explains many things.
No, I have no desire to know what, or who I was once;
or what, or who, I shall be in the ages to come.
This belief in immortality makes present living
the more attractive. It gives you all the time there is.
You will always be able to finish what you start.
There is no fever or strain in such an outlook.
We are here in life for one purpose—to get experience.
We are all getting it, and we shall all use it somewhere.
—Henry Ford

> No honest theologian therefore can deny
> that his acceptance of Jesus as Christ logically binds
> every Christian to a belief in reincarnation
> —in Elias's case (who was later John the Baptist) at least.
> —Robert Graves

> There is no death.
> How can there be death if everything is part of the Godhead?
> The soul never dies and the body is never really alive.
> —Isaac Bashevis Singer

Summary of the Principle of Oneness

A. The Universe is 95 percent unknown.
B. Everything is an infinite field of energy.
C. This field of energy is known as the Universe/God.
D. All energy and matter is identical at its subatomic core.
E. Everything has a degree of consciousness.
F. The collective consciousness controls and manifests everything.
G. The Universe/God energy field transcends space and time.
H. The Universe/God energy field is in a constant state of change.

2. The Key Aspects of God/the Universe

A. There Are Many Misconceptions Regarding God/the Universe

The concept of God, the Universe, the Divine or its other names is widely discussed but seldom understood. God is not separate from man and the physical world but rather is the collective of "all that is." Religions have attempted to define God in human terms. These attempts, known as anthropomorphism, attribute human qualities or form to a deity. Efforts to humanize God/the Universe are problematic—they limit an entity that is infinite in nature. Conversely, pantheism is the belief that the universe and nature in its totality, is the Divine and that God is an impersonal entity. Both anthropomorphism and pantheism are an incomplete understanding of God/the Universe.

So is God/the Universe a personal entity? Does God take human form and live, breath and emote like humans? The answer is both yes and no. The Universe/God can be personal or impersonal, depending upon the thoughts and beliefs of the individual branches of consciousness wishing to experience God/the Universe. We humans are in many respects the personal aspects of God/the Universe, however in the scheme of things we represent a very small part of "all that is." There are many more realms where the field of energy extends that do not include human consciousness. I would argue that God/the Universe is both pantheistic and anthropomorphic. By simple logical analysis, if something is "all that is," it must be inclusive of both pantheism and anthropomorphism. God/the Universe expresses itself in both personal and impersonal facets. It is both animated humans and inanimate rocks. Regardless of the form, God/the Universe is a creation of the collective consciousness and not the other way around. Swami Vivekananda explains the source and location of God/the Universe in this revealing quote.

> There is no God separate from you,
> no God higher than you, the real "you."
> All the gods are little beings to you,
> all the ideas of God and Father in heaven are
> but your own reflection. God Himself is your image.
> "God created man after His own image." That is wrong.
> Man creates God after his own image. That is right.

> Throughout the universe we are creating gods
> after our own image.
> We create the god and fall down at his feet and worship him;
> and when this dream comes, we love it!
> —Swami Vivekananda

Albert Einstein struggled with the notion that our minds may be too limited to grasp the concept of God/the Universe. In an interview published in 1930, he answered a question about whether he considered himself as a pantheist.

> Your question is the most difficult in the world.
> It is not a question I can answer simply with yes or no.
> I am not an Atheist.
> I do not know if I can define myself as a Pantheist.
> The problem involved is too vast for our limited minds.
> May I not reply with a parable?
> The human mind, no matter how highly trained,
> cannot grasp the universe. We are in the position of a little child,
> entering a huge library whose walls are covered to the ceiling
> with books in many different tongues.
> The child knows that someone must have written those books.
> It does not know who or how.
> It does not understand the languages in which they are written.
> The child notes a definite plan in the arrangement of the books,
> a mysterious order, which it does not comprehend,
> but only dimly suspects. That, it seems to me,
> is the attitude of the human mind,
> even the greatest and most cultured, toward God.

> We see a universe marvelously arranged, obeying certain laws,
> but we understand the laws only dimly. Our limited minds
> cannot grasp the mysterious force that sways the constellations.
> I am fascinated by Spinoza's Pantheism.
> I admire even more his contributions to modern thought.
> Spinoza is the greatest of modern philosophers,
> because he is the first philosopher who deals with
> the soul and the body as one,
> not as two separate things.
> —Albert Einstein

It is worth your time to reexamine your thoughts and beliefs of who and what God/the Universe is. Keeping an open mind, you may come to a much deeper understanding of the true nature of God/the Universe. It may also require suspending or transcending the thought process itself to experience something that cannot adequately be explained by words.

B. God/the Universe Is Within Us

In searching for God/the Universe, do not seek outward but rather seek inward, in the stillness of your being. God/the Universe is synonymous with the collective consciousness, which is responsible for the creation of everything physical. Our individual consciousness is a branch of the collective consciousness, but we often are unaware of our connection. When people find God, Jesus or the Divine, they are merely allowing the connection that was always there. You are God/the Universe both in part and totality, and you should realize your control of and connection to everything. Jesus attempted to explain this to his persecutors.

> The Jews took up stones again to stone him. Jesus replied,
> "I have shown you many good works from the Father.
> For which of these are you going to stone me?"
> The Jews answered,
> "It is not for a good work that we are going to stone you,
> but for blasphemy, because you, though only a human being,
> are making yourself God."
> Jesus answered, "Is it not written in your law,
> 'I said, you are gods'?
> If those to whom the word of God came were called 'gods'
> —and the scripture cannot be annulled
> —can you say that the one whom the Father has sanctified
> and sent into the world is blaspheming because I said,
> 'I am God's Son'?
> If I am not doing the works of my Father,
> then do not believe me.
> But if I do them, even though you do not believe me,
> believe the works, so that you may know and understand
> that the Father is in me and I am in the Father."
> Then they tried to arrest him again,
> but he escaped from their hands.
> —John 10:31-40 (NRSV)

Jesus says "you are gods" and that "the Father is in me and I am in the Father." This is a literal instance of Jesus explaining that we are gods and that the Divine energy force (the Father) is omnipresent within us while we are also omnipresent within God.

Rumi also made this profound point about the omnipresence of God/the Universe and its relationship to man, in his very succinct quote.

> You are not a drop in the ocean.
> You are the entire ocean,
> in a drop.
> — Rumi

The ocean symbolizes God/the Universe. Rumi is revealing that we are not an insignificant part (drop) of God/the Universe but rather that all of God/the Universe is contained within us. The Divine energy field is everywhere, and we are part as well as all of it. This is an enormous concept to comprehend.

A similar illustration of this concept of God/the Universe within us is the inner potential for variation of human stem cells. Human stem cells contain all possible cell variations and can become any type of cell necessary. This is an example of the Principle of Oneness; because within each seemingly separate part; is the entire Universe with all possible variations. Everything has the ability to be anyone or anything because you quite literally are all the other variations along with your individual identity. The Universe/God code exists in even the minutest speck of sand.

We are multidimensional beings and exist everywhere and at every time.

> Stop acting so small.
> You are the universe in ecstatic motion.
> —Rumi

> The universe is but one vast Symbol of God.
> —Thomas Carlyle

> I searched for God and found only myself.
> I searched for myself and found only God.
> —Sufi proverb

C. God/the Universe Is a Democracy of One

If we are all multiple personalities of God/the Universe, who is in charge? Is the collective consciousness a democracy or a dictatorship? What about the religious views of God in control and humans being merely servants doing God's work? Control is everywhere in the collective consciousness and exists in every cell in your body and every atom of every facet of the Universe. We are all in charge, and we all are directing the Universe through the collective consciousness. All the various facets or branches of personal consciousness are voting with their thoughts and beliefs to slow energy and create the physical realities. It is a democracy of one multiple personality, sometimes in harmony and sometimes in conflict.

Harmony is creation and disharmony is destruction. Because we are often unaware of how large we actually are, we are consequently unaware of all our thoughts and beliefs within our broader collective consciousness.

Know that you are God/the Universe and that anywhere you aim/focus your consciousness you create reality in one of the infinite physical and nonphysical realms. It all begins with thought, contemplation, prayer, dreams, plans, desires or any method of focusing your consciousness. If you wish to praise or blame God/the Universe for something, you should do it in a mirror. It is you and has always been you in charge of all reality.

Summary of the Key Aspects of God/the Universe

A. **There Are Many Misconceptions Regarding God/the Universe**
Most religions have only a limited understanding of God/the Universe. God/the Universe is "all that is," and this includes both pantheism (impersonal) and anthropomorphism (personal) expressions of the Divine.

B. **God/the Universe Is Within Us**
In searching for God/the Universe, do not seek outward, but rather seek inward. All answers come from within because we are simultaneously both part and all, of the energy of God/the Universe.

C. **God/the Universe Is a Democracy of One**
We are a multi-personality, multidimensional being existing everywhere and in every time. Our collective consciousness is in charge, co-creating the illusion of reality through the various branches of individual consciousness.

3. Living the Principle of Oneness

Intellectually understanding the Principle of Oneness may not ensure enlightenment if you cannot actually feel and experience Oneness. Truly experiencing Oneness involves recognizing and allowing meaningful, loving connections with your broader self. This includes experiencing loving connections with all aspects of the Universe/God, not just people but also nature, places, food, music, art, activities and much more. These connections are naturally there, but we often fail to realize them or sometimes reject them. When you truly love anyone or anything, you are acknowledging your Oneness with it, and on an emotional level it can feel profoundly blissful and euphoric.

Experiencing Oneness involves employing wisdom to see beyond the illusion of separateness. There are at least two essential actions to experience the Principle of Oneness.

1. **Know the magnitude of who and what you are.**
2. **Choose to love every facet of yourself unconditionally.**

These are no small tasks, but chances are many of us have had flashes of Oneness at various times in our lives. Honest expressions of love are the epitome of Oneness.

1. Know the magnitude of who and what you are.

You are both part and all the Universe/God, and you are in control of everything. You are also at least three distinct yet connected parts: the illusion of the physical body, the mind or branch of personal consciousness and the energy of the collective consciousness, which is the soul/Universe/God. Recognize these three parts, then allow and expand the connections to everything and experience Oneness.

> Enlightenment is the complete flowering
> of body, mind and the soul.
> —Amit Ray

> Knowing others is Wisdom,
> knowing yourself is Enlightenment
> —Lao Tzu

> Your own Self-Realization
> is the greatest service you can render the world.
> —Ramana Maharshi

> Your greatest awakening comes,
> when you are aware about your infinite nature.
> —Amit Ray

> There are three things extremely hard:
> steel, a diamond, and to know one's self.
> —Benjamin Franklin

> One's own self is well hidden from one's own self;
> of all mines of treasure,
> one's own is the last to be dug up.
> —Friedrich Wilhelm Nietzsche

> Knowing yourself is the beginning of all wisdom.
> —Aristotle

A. See yourself in everything and everyone.

You quite literally are everything and everyone, yet may not be aware of it or behave as such. On a daily basis you can choose to treat everything you encounter as the extension of yourself. View the entire Universe and everyone and everything in it with love and without judgement, lest you want judge or hate yourself. The Universe longs to experience its natural Oneness through the simple act of love.

> He who experiences the unity of life
> sees his own Self in all beings.
> —Buddha

> In each of us there is another whom we do not know.
> —Carl Jung

> We live in everyone. I live in you. You live in me.
> There is no gap, no distance.
> —Amit Ray

> And suddenly you realize:
> you are in every dot of the universe vanishing and arising.
> —Amit Ray

Every person and everything is an extension of your consciousness. This includes humans, animals, elements of nature, inanimate objects and everything down to a subatomic level. You have manifested them and they have manifested you through the collective consciousness. On a higher spiritual level, we strive for individuality, then later long to reconnect with ourselves in a never-ending cycle. We long to know every aspect of our broader self because this is the act of self-realization. Our self-realization is recognizing that we are both branches of the Universe/God as well as the entire tree of collective consciousness.

> Each person you meet is an aspect of yourself,
> clamoring for love.
> —Eric Micha'el Leventhal

> All differences in this world are of degree, and not of kind,
> because oneness is the secret of everything.
> —Swami Vivekananda

If you see yourself in everyone and everything, you will naturally strive for win/win scenarios in all aspects of life. If you wish well for others, you are manifesting success for your broader self. You have the opportunity to be kind, loving and helpful to yourself and your various facets/incarnations, which will bring peace, joy and happiness to you and the collective consciousness.

> We all are so deeply interconnected;
> we have no option but to love all.
> Be kind and do good for any one and that will be reflected.
> The ripples of the kind heart
> are the highest blessings of the Universe.
> —Amit Ray

> Do not neglect to show hospitality to strangers,
> for by doing that
> some have entertained angels without knowing it.
> —Hebrews 13:2 (NRSV)

When you realize you are the Universe/God, you also realize that your individual ego's desires (your branch of personal consciousness) may not be the most important if it comes at the cost of hurting other aspects of yourself or something else. Even in a win or lose scenario, your individual ego's losing could provide a positive win scenario for another aspect of yourself that may need the win more. The enlightenment of Oneness is realizing that your sacrifice of losing could be for the greater good of the collective consciousness/ the Universe/God.

> There is only one all pervading God.
> It has only one message:
> love all, encompass all and transcend
> the limits of the selfish gene.
> —Amit Ray

You also have the option to be mean, hateful and harmful to yourself and the various facets/incarnations of yourself that will yield pain, suffering and unhappiness. If you desire ill will or harm to others, you are manifesting harm to your broader self. The Universe/God allows both positive and negative choices without judgement or punishment. Make your choices consciously and wisely. Because, depending upon the choice, your own consciousness may reward or punish yourself. The nonjudgement of the Universe/God is explained in greater detail in the Principle of Neutrality and Nonjudgement.

> You will not be punished for your anger;
> you will be punished by your anger.
> —Buddha

When you chose to harm another aspect of yourself, it requires a willing victim to receive the hurt. This victim is another aspect of your consciousness that is projecting a belief of a victim, either consciously or unconsciously. If you believe you are weak, powerless, always taken advantage of or even just unlucky, you are susceptible to participate as a victim in these scenarios. That part of your consciousness, through your thoughts and beliefs, is signaling the Universe/God that you wish to experience being a victim. Your thoughts, desires and emotions can create matter and situations in the physical realities. Be very mindful of what and where your consciousness goes and how you are thinking at all times. It may be better to proactively place positive thoughts in your consciousness rather than pick up random, unwanted negative thoughts from your environment.

Seeing yourself in everything also means realizing you are one with nature, animals, the sky, the ocean, art, music, dance, architecture, activities, food—everything. You have the opportunity to reconnect and experience the enjoyment and energy of these other physical aspects of yourself. This is one of the great pleasures of experiencing the physical realm versus experiencing the spiritual, nonphysical realm. This explains that sense of awe when we look out into the vastness of the sky, or the depth of an ocean, or the beauty of the forest and mountains. When we look out into the world, we are looking into a mirror. On a higher spiritual level, we recognize our Oneness with everything and are amazed.

> We know that God is everywhere;
> but certainly we feel His presence most
> when His works are on the grandest scale spread before us;
> and it is in the unclouded night-sky,
> where His worlds wheel their silent course,
> that we read clearest His infinitude,
> His omnipotence, His omnipresence.
> —Charlotte Brontë

> There are only two ways to live your life.
> One is as though nothing is a miracle.
> The other is as though everything is a miracle.
> —Albert Einstein

> Our task must be to free ourselves
> by widening our circle of compassion
> to embrace all living creatures
> and the whole of nature and its beauty.
> —Albert Einstein

> The world is full of magic things,
> patiently waiting for our senses to grow sharper.
> —William Butler Yeats

> The invariable mark of wisdom
> is to see the miraculous in the common.
> —Ralph Waldo Emerson

> There is a pleasure in the pathless woods,
> There is a rapture on the lonely shore,
> There is society, where none intrudes,
> By the deep sea, and music in its roar:
> I love not man the less, but Nature more.
> —George Gordon Byron

B. Transcend the limits of the personal ego.

The personal ego identifies with a very limited part of the self and prevents you from recognizing the largeness of who you really are. When you let go of your ego and selfishness, you realize you are both part and all of everything. When you let go of the personal ego, you will begin to see the big picture of the Universe/God. You will understand that your ego's desires may not be what are best for the Universe/God/collective consciousness. You will have the wisdom to freely sacrifice personal desires for the greater good of your broader self.

> Stop acting so small.
> You are the universe in ecstatic motion.
> —Rumi

The true value of a human being can be found
in the degree to which he has attained
liberation from the self.
—Albert Einstein

The most common ego identifications
have to do with possessions, the work you do,
social status and recognition, knowledge and education,
physical appearance, special abilities, relationships,
person and family history, belief systems,
and often nationalistic, racial, religious,
and other collective identifications.
None of these is you.
—Eckhart Tolle

Forget the self and you will fear nothing,
in whatever level or awareness
you find yourself to be.
—Carlos Castaneda

The weak are dominated by their ego,
the wise dominate their ego,
and the intelligent
are in a constant struggle against their ego.
—Hamza Yusuf

When I had nothing to lose,
I had everything.
When I stopped being who I am,
I found myself.
—Paulo Coelho

Enlightenment is ego's ultimate disappointment.
—Chogyam Trungpa

C. Realize you are eternal and transcend space and time.

Our Oneness exists in infinite multiple realities and infinite time periods simultaneously. At our core we are pure energy that cannot be created or destroyed and that transcends space and time. We are constantly directing our consciousness in different scenarios and realities. Sometimes we redirect ourselves and close a chapter with the apparent death or destruction of someone or something. This matter is just converted back to its original, faster vibrating spiritual energy. Nothing ever dies, but the physical illusion is no longer in front of us. This physical illusion does still exist in another dimension, but our consciousness has shifted its attention away from that dimension. It is like leaving one room in a house and moving into another. When we move to another room, the previous room remains intact with everyone and everything. We are all of our past, present and future lives, as well as the younger and older versions of ourselves. We are also every version, of everyone, in every time, everywhere. Space and time are collective illusions, and we exist in these other dimensions and times for eternity. Your broader self can and does signal your personal consciousness from other times, other places and other dimensions. Ghosts, deceased relatives, channeled entities, psychic connections and communication with God are all examples of your broader self signaling your personal consciousness. Everything in the physical world is a signal and a sign from the spiritual energy of the collective consciousness.

> Time is not at all what it seems to be.
> It is not flowing in one direction,
> and the future exists simultaneously with the past.
> —Albert Einstein

> All of your past selves are walking behind you,
> like a shadow, waiting for you to awaken fully.
> Waiting for you to return home. To the Oneness.
> To love, wisdom, silence and compassion.
> The child you once were is still with you.
> It is waiting to receive the unconditional love
> and acceptance which it has always wanted
> which will finally heal it, calm it and enable it to relax
> and surrender into the vastness of your Being.
> Into the light of consciousness.
> And it is not just the child who is walking behind you.
> All the identities from past incarnations are still with you.
> The seeker. The pirate. The highwayman. The sage.
> —Leonard Jacobson

> To the extent that we even understand string theory,
> it may imply a massive number of possible different universes
> with different laws of physics in each universe,
> and there may be no way of distinguishing between them
> or saying why the laws of physics are the way they are.
> —Lawrence M. Krauss

> The universe bursts into existence from life,
> not the other way around as we have been taught.
> For each life there is a universe, its own universe.
> We generate spheres of reality,
> individual bubbles of existence.
> Our planet is comprised of billions of spheres of reality,
> generated by each individual human
> and perhaps even by each animal.
> —Robert Lanza

D. Seek all answers and all change from within.

We have access to all knowledge and wisdom of the Universe/God through our connection to the collective consciousness. Once you fully embrace Oneness with the Universe/God, you will look inward through your personal consciousness to the collective consciousness for all answers. You may find yourself drawn to the wisdom of other beings from various periods in history such as Buddha, Rumi and Einstein. Know that this is still you connecting to another aspect of yourself. If you solicit advice or help from others facets of yourself, you should still confirm within your personal consciousness and the collective consciousness to determine whether the answers ring true. You are the ultimate authority on all knowledge and wisdom, you just may be unaware or afraid to trust the answers within. This also means recognizing the external signs of the physical world as reflections of the state of your broader consciousness. Recognize that you are signaling yourself and interpret the signals as such. Your signals (the physical world) are not where you should go, but where you currently are, based upon your present state of consciousness. Changes in anyone's life always come from changes within their personal consciousness and the collective consciousness.

If you like where you are in life, continue believing and thinking as you are. If you wish for something different, shift and redirect your thoughts and beliefs within your personal consciousness. Make different choices within your consciousness. Only those parts of the collective consciousness with strong, non-conflicting inner visions change the physical world. They simply *will* things into existence.

Personal responsibility for everything is the hallmark of an enlightened being. If you blame others, bad luck or the Universe/God for your difficulties, you clearly do not understand the Principle of Oneness. You are in charge and responsible for everything. Embrace your power and make no excuses.

> Yesterday I was so cleaver,
> so I wanted to change the world.
> Today I am so wise,
> so I am changing myself.
> —Rumi

Everything in the universe is within you.
Ask all from yourself.
—Rumi

Peace comes from within. Do not seek it without.
—Buddha

All wonders you seek are within yourself.
—Sir Thomas Browne

Your vision will become clear
only when you can look into your own heart.
Who looks outside, dreams;
who looks inside, awakes.
—Carl Jung

Quotes Worth Repeating from the Introduction

Enlightenment is man's release
from his self-incurred tutelage.
Tutelage is man's inability to make use
of his understanding without direction from another.
Self-incurred is this tutelage when its cause lies
not in lack of reason but in lack of resolution
and courage to use it without direction from another.
Sapere aude! "Have courage to use your own reason!"
—that is the motto of enlightenment.
—Immanuel Kant

> "I shall no longer be instructed by the Yoga Veda
> or the Aharva Veda, or the ascetics,
> or any other doctrine whatsoever.
> I shall learn from myself, be a pupil of myself;
> I shall get to know myself, the mystery of Siddhartha."
> He looked around as if he were seeing the world
> for the first time.
> —Hermann Hesse

> Enlightenment means
> taking full responsibility for your life.
> —William Blake

2. Choose to love every facet of yourself unconditionally.

You are a complex, multidimensional being and loving yourself requires identifying, accepting and loving all of our seemingly separate parts. This includes your personal self, broader self (other people), balance of the physical world (nature, activities, concepts…) and the collective Universe/God. It is also important to identify and transcend all negative emotions. These negative emotions are helpful signals that something is out of sync with your consciousness and in conflict with the unity of Oneness.

A. Love yourself (your personal consciousness) unconditionally.

The single most important relationship you have is with yourself; when you realize you are everything, your relationship with yourself can become an infinite expression of love. How you treat and view yourself (personal consciousness) may dictate how you interact with the rest of yourself, the Universe/God. If you hate yourself, you will hate others. If you love yourself, you will love others. If you are hard on yourself, you will be hard on others. If you are compassionate with yourself, you will be compassionate with others. Love, respect, unconditionally accept, and encourage yourself to the greatest of your abilities. Either love who you are and where you are—relishing this moment—or love where you are going and who you will become, delighting in your path. Allow nothing to interfere with your sacred relationship with yourself and strive to maintain an unshakeable sense of self-confidence.

> You, yourself, as much as anybody in the entire universe,
> deserve your love and affection.
> —Buddha

> The most terrifying thing is to accept oneself completely.
> —Carl Jung

> Dare to love yourself
> as if you were a rainbow with gold at both ends.
> —Aberjhani

> The most powerful relationship you will ever have
> is the relationship with yourself.
> —Steve Maraboli

> It's surprising how many persons go through life
> without ever recognizing that their feelings toward other people
> are largely determined by their feelings toward themselves,
> and if you're not comfortable within yourself,
> you can't be comfortable with others.
> —Sidney J. Harris

B. Love your broader self (other people) unconditionally.

Regarding the other facets of yourself, you have a least two distinctive choices in life. The first choice is to connect to your broader self with acceptance and love. The other option is to ignore the profound connections and react with indifference, fear or even hate. Both choices are acceptable to the Universe/God. The collective consciousness does not judge itself. The Universe/God also does not disconnect from what we have labeled as bad or evil. The Universe/God allows all expressions regardless of their form or behavior. When you choose honest, loving connections, you will feel emotionally blissful; if you make hateful choices, you will feel unpleasantness and pain. A great goal each day is to have as many meaningful, loving connections with your broader self as possible.

Why do we cry at others misfortune or smile at their success? Why are we sometimes brought to tears when we witness a victorious athlete become emotional? Why do we feel discomfort when we watch someone suffer? We empathize with them, and both empathy and compassion are emotional revelations of Oneness. On a higher level, you recognize your connection and realize that the person is actually part of you. Actively cultivate your empathy and compassion for others to experience the Principle of Oneness. Be careful when empathizing with other's pain/suffering so you do not absorb their burden unless that is your actual desire. View the pain of the world as the illusion that it is. It is a personal spiritual choice to experience a situation. Pain and suffering can be a conscious choice, but it is more often an unconscious choice created by negative thoughts and beliefs.

It is easy to love the facets of yourself that you have judged to be beautiful, talented or successful. But how do you respond or interact with difficult aspects of yourself? What do you do when you cross paths with someone angry, sad, depressed, illogical, violent, radical, selfish, mean, negative, pessimistic or hateful? First pause and acknowledge their behavior as a reflection of you own inner issues. Don't take anything personally, but do contemplate why you brought forth and chose to participate in this situation. What do you have to gain from this or what do you wish to experience?

If you feel insecure or unhappy, you will be drawn to or create someone who may treat you poorly. Your thoughts, beliefs and emotions are like orders at a restaurant and the Universe/God will serve up whatever you request through your state of mind. Pay attention to your thoughts, beliefs, emotions and words because you are placing orders that you may or may not actually want.

We are a complex and complicated, multidimensional being. Whoever crosses your path each day is another part of yourself you need to see or meet that day. Greet them with love and respect, and be open to give or receive. You can choose to be pleasant and strive for a meaningful connection. Put your focus on them and not just on yourself. A simple greeting, smile, eye contact, kind word or kind gestures are all appropriate. Ignoring, aggressive, angry, demanding, selfish gestures are acts of disconnection. Look at others as you might a small child: with kindness, openness, sweetness, awe and love. You are signaling yourself constantly with the people and situations you have co-created through the collective consciousness.

> When you adopt the viewpoint
> that there is nothing that exists that is not part of you,
> that there is no one who exists who is not part of you,
> that any judgment you make is self-judgment,
> that any criticism you level is self-criticism,
> you will wisely extend to yourself
> an unconditional love
> that will be the light of the world.
> —Harry Palmer

> So then, the relationship of self to other
> is the complete realization that loving yourself
> is impossible without loving everything
> defined as other than yourself.
> —Alan W. Watts

Variations of the Golden Rule in Philosophy and Religion

Hurt not others in ways that you yourself would find hurtful.
—Udanavarga 5:18 (Buddhism)

> In everything do to others as you would have them do to you;
> for this is the law and the prophets.
> —Matthew 7:12 NRSV (Christianity)

> Do not do to others what you would not like yourself.
> —Analects 15:23 (Confucianism)

> This is the sum of Dharma (duty): Do naught onto others
> which would cause you pain if done to you.
> —Mahabharata 5:1517 (Hinduism)

> None of you [truly] believes until he wishes for his brother
> what he wishes for himself.
> —An-Nawawi's Forty Hadith 13 (Islam)

> What is hateful to you, do not do to your fellowman.
> This is the entire Law; all the rest is commentary.
> —Talmud, Shabbat 31a (Judaism)

> Regard your neighbor's gain as your gain,
> and your neighbor's loss as your own loss.
> —Tai Shang Kan Yin P'ien (Taoism)

C. Love the nonhuman aspects of the Universe/God.

Oneness with the Universe/God also includes connecting with and the love of animals, plants, all of nature, inanimate objects and abstract concepts. We can and do experience great joy when we connect with nature, food, drink, art, music, dance and architecture. Even loving abstract things and concepts such as freedom, liberty, knowledge, activities, hobbies and travel are part of the Principle of Oneness. When you lovingly connect with any of these, you are rediscovering aspects of yourself. Everything down to the subatomic level has a degree of consciousness and it all longs to experience and reconnect to the collective.

Loving a sport, music, knowledge, learning, personal growth, all help to connect with the broader self, which again is the Universe/God. You have the choice to love and connect with anything you desire and experience joy and happiness through this process. People have called this finding your passion or finding your bliss, and it is one of the keys to creating happiness in life.

Be absorbed in an interesting work of art. Immerse yourself in the story of a great book. Be mesmerized by a colorful sunset. Be in the zone of your favorite sport. Become one with the ball. Just do it! Lose yourself in a movie. Fight for a cause important to you. Express your passion for justice. Savor your favorite food. Delight in an intellectual achievement. Gaze in awe at the vast ocean. Contemplate the infinite night sky. Respect and cherish mother earth. Deeply inhale a breath of fresh air. Love your dog, cat, horse or any animal or pet. Enjoy your sexuality. All of these are some of the infinite number of expressions of Oneness. Be guided by your own preferences of what to love and connect with. There are no right or wrong choices, but your preferences will determine your enjoyment of the loving connection.

If your list of things you love is short, you probably also have shortages of self-love. If your list of things you hate is long, you probably also have long lists of things you hate about yourself. Again, the Universe/God allows all choices, but you decide which choice feels better and you wish to continue.

> This is a subtle truth:
> whatever you love, you are.
> —Rumi

> I do believe in an everyday sort of magic
> —the inexplicable connectedness we sometimes experience
> with places, people, works of art and the like;
> the eerie appropriateness of moments of synchronicity;
> the whispered voice, the hidden presence,
> when we think we're alone.
> —Charles de Lint

> I only went out for a walk
> and finally concluded to stay out till sundown,
> for going out,
> I found, was really going in.
> —John Muir

> The clearest way into the Universe
> is through a forest wilderness.
> —John Muir

D. Love God/the Universe.

When you love and connect with God/the Universe, you are aligning your personal consciousness with the entire collective energy field/God rather than just connecting with smaller parts of the energy field or other personal consciousnesses. Worshipping, praying, speaking to or hearing from God; are all ways to experience the Principle of Oneness. Communicate with God/the Universe daily. Talk, dream, project, plan, or, better yet, emotionally believe what you desire and that reality will manifest with the force of the entire energy field. Project your feelings of love, hope, joy, optimism, peace or whatever you desire to God/the Universe. God is the entire collective consciousness and voice of your broader, higher self. God is the entire energy field where our individual consciousness branches from and remains connected to. You are in God, and all of God is in you. When you talk to yourself, you are talking to God/the Universe. When you talk to God/the Universe, you are taking to yourself. Loving yourself is synonymous with loving God/the Universe. Loving God/the Universe is an act of reconnecting, self-discovery, self-acceptance and self-love. The Principle of Oneness is the recognition of the Divine in everyone and everything.

> Love is the reflection of God's unity in the world of duality.
> It constitutes the entire significance of creation.
> —Meher Baba

> Whoever does not love does not know God,
> for God is love.
> —John 4:8 (NRSV)

> God loves each of us as if there were only one of us.
> —Saint Augustine

> Teacher, which commandment in the law is the greatest?
> He said to him, "You shall love the Lord your God
> with all your heart, and with all your soul,
> and with all your mind."
> This is the greatest and first commandment.
> And a second is like it:
> "You shall love your neighbor as yourself."
> On these two commandments
> hang all the law and the prophets.
> —Jesus, Matthew 22:36-40 (NRSV)

E. Identify and transcend all negative feelings of hate, indifference, anger, dislike, embarrassment or any emotion that feels unpleasant.

All negative emotions will feel unpleasant, and that is your indication that something is out of balance with the Universe/God. All emotions that feel unpleasant are signals of inconsistencies within the collective consciousness. These inconsistencies are often false beliefs of duality in the Universe/God and in opposition to the natural unity of the Principle of Oneness. If you attack or wish ill of someone, you are attaching and sabotaging yourself. If you hate others, you hate yourself. Instead of reacting with dislike or hate, choose instead to just allow that part of you to exist without any judgement. This is the enlightened choice.

> Hate hurts the hater more'n the hated.
> —Madeleine L'Engle

> When you really know somebody you can't hate them.
> Or maybe it's just that you can't really know them
> until you stop hating them.
> —Orson Scott Card

> The opposite of love is not hate, it's apathy,
> when you simply don't bother about that person!
> —Amish Tripathi

> Holding on to anger is like grasping a hot coal
> with the intent of throwing it at someone else;
> you are the one who gets burned.
> —Buddha

> Try to understand men.
> If you understand each other you will be kind to each other.
> Knowing a man well never leads to hate
> and almost always leads to love.
> —John Steinbeck

Summary of Living the Principle of Oneness

1. **Know the magnitude of who and what you are.**
   A. See yourself in everything and everyone.
   B. Transcend the limits of the personal ego.
   C. Realize you are eternal and transcend space and time.
   D. Seek all answers and all change from within.

2. **Choose to love every facet of yourself unconditionally.**
   A. Love yourself (your personal consciousness) unconditionally.
   B. Love your broader self (other people) unconditionally.
   C. Love the nonhuman aspects of the Universe/God.
   D. Love God/the Universe.
   E. Identify and transcend all negative feelings.

Conclusion

Every living being is an engine
geared to the wheelwork of the universe.
Though seemingly affected only by its immediate surrounding,
the sphere of external influence extends to infinite distance.
—Nikola Tesla

A human being is a part of the whole,
called by us "Universe,"
a part limited in time and space.
He experiences himself, his thoughts and feelings
as something separated from the rest
—a kind of optical delusion of his consciousness.
The striving to free oneself from this delusion
is the one issue of true religion.
Not to nourish the delusion
but to try to overcome it
is the way to reach the attainable measure
of peace of mind.
—Albert Einstein

We are all profoundly interconnected and part of one infinite entity. We take joy in exploring and connecting with our other parts and broader self. We are in a constant state of flux, alternating from the appearance of many and back to the true reality of Oneness. Our collective consciousness allows us to form any reality we wish. If we chose to ignore and reject our Oneness, we experience loneliness, unhappiness and pain. However, when we recognize, trust and live Oneness, we experience happiness, love and joyfulness. Truly experiencing the Principle Oneness is all about recognizing and allowing meaningful, loving connections with your broader self. Enlightenment is realizing you are everyone, everything, everywhere at every time.

Special Message to the Reader

If you appreciate the truth and wisdom of this book, keep it as a reference guide on your path to enlightenment. Use *The Principle of Oneness* as a key to interpret other works of wisdom, helping to unlock their deeper meanings. Live and experience your Oneness with the Universe, and feel the joy and bliss that results. Help spread the word by sharing this knowledge. Speak with others, or submit a book review that notes how these principles can enrich your life. Gift a copy of this book to anyone you believe could benefit from its knowledge and wisdom. One of the greatest things we can do is to inspire others.

Thank you for helping enlighten the world.

Russell Anthony Gibbs

RussellAnthonyGibbs.com

About the Author

AWARD-WINNING AND BESTSELLING AUTHOR RUSSELL Anthony Gibbs is a philosopher and spiritual seeker on a quest for enlightenment. His critically acclaimed first book, ***The Six Principles of Enlightenment and Meaning of Life***, won the 2016 Pinnacle Book Achievement Award for Best Book in Spiritual Self Help. *The Six Principles* is a comprehensive overview of the fundamentals of enlightenment and is the first of an eight-book series. This book, ***The Principle of Oneness***, is the second in the series.

Gibbs grew up in a huge family—he is one of eleven children—on a farm in Iowa. A rebellious child, Gibbs was kicked out of Catholic elementary school in sixth grade. Early in life, he began questioning the teachings of Catholicism and struggled to understand his relationship with God and the meaning of life. The information from two channeled entities, Seth and Abraham profoundly influences Gibbs. His research into Baha'ism, Buddhism, Christianity, Judaism, Hinduism, Islam, Sufism and Taoism also greatly influence his spiritual and philosophical perspective. He incorporates quantum mechanics, physics and psychology as well as concepts from the works of Albert Einstein, Carl Jung, Sigmund Freud and Stephen Hawking.

Gibbs's communication style is concise, intense and deep. He would rather express wisdom in brief, powerful quotes and concise paragraphs rather than in complicated, long-winded explanations. Espresso Wisdom is short, strong, rich insight. Like espresso coffee, it gives an intense jolt of enlightenment. Enlightenment is an awakening, and Espresso Wisdom is meant to help jumpstart you on your journey.

Espresso Wisdom ☕
Short, Strong, Rich Insight! ™

Acknowledgments

In the spirit of *The Principle of Oneness*, I wish to acknowledge the other aspects of myself and the collective consciousness for their ability to articulate profound wisdom in such a way that helped me understand and write this book. I express my gratitude to the following people and entities who have greatly inspired me along my path.

Jane Roberts and her series of channeled books entitled ***Seth Speaks***, for showing me a wealth of profound information on the true nature of our reality.

Buddha, the founder of Buddhism, whose personal quest for enlightenment has illuminated my path with truth, wisdom and peace of mind. His succinct quotes are powerful, rich, insightful and completely accessible even today, thousands of years after his death.

Albert Einstein was one of the greatest minds in the history of mankind. His quotes speak to me with profound knowledge and clarity. I am in awe with his ability to articulate extremely complex concepts so simply.

Rumi, a Persian thirteenth-century poet and Sufi, so beautifully expressed wisdom that it is not surprising he is one of the most-read poets in the world. Some of Rumi's quotes are so incredibly simple yet so unbelievably deep that they have guided me effortlessly toward enlightenment.

Jesus Christ represents the emotional, devotional side of enlightenment for me. The Christian principles of love and forgiveness help to complete the wisdom of the circle of enlightenment.

Ester Hicks and her channeled material from the entity **Abraham** have provided me meaningful and practical information on the Principle of Manifestation.

Louise L. Hay is the quintessential guide for self-healing and physical-body manifestations. I continue to use her book *You Can Heal Yourself* as a guide to resolving any issues in my body.

Brian L. Weiss's book on reincarnation *Many Lives, Many Masters* opened my eyes to the multiple dimensions and lives of our existence. His work has shaped my understanding of the cycle of life and has provided a sense of peace and understanding that our existence is eternal.

Index of Quoted Authors and Sacred Texts

Sacred Text References

The Upanishads (written between 800 BC-200 BC) A collection of texts that contain some of the central philosophical concepts of Hinduism, some of which are shared with Buddhism, Jainism and Sikhism

The Bhagavad Gita (written between 300 BC–AD 300) Literally "Song of the Lord," Hindu scripture in Sanskrit that is part of the epic Mahabharata, a narrative of the Kurukshetra War and the fates of the Kaurava and the Pandava princes

The New Revised Standard Version (NRSV) An English translation of the Christian Bible from the Vulgate released in 1989 and is an updated revision of the Revised Standard Version (which was itself an update of the American Standard Version)

The Udanavarga An early Buddhist collection containing topically organized chapters of aphoristic verses and statements attributed to the Buddha and his disciples

The Analects (475 BC–221 BC) A collection of sayings and ideas attributed to the Chinese philosopher Confucius and his contemporaries

The Mahabharata (300 BC–AD 300) An epic narrative of the Kurukshetra War and the fates of the Kaurava and the Pandava princes, including the Bhagavad Gita, the story of Damayanti, an abbreviated version of the Ramayana and the Rishyasringa

Nawawi's Forty, a compilation of forty hadiths of the Koran by Imam al- Nawawī (1233–1277), one of the most eminent and revered authorities in Islamic jurisprudence that explains the foundations of Shari'a (Islamic "sacred war")

The Talmud (200 BCE–500 CE) A central text of Rabbinic Judaism containing the teachings and opinions of thousands of rabbis on a variety of subjects, including Halakha (law), Jewish ethics, philosophy, customs, history, lore and many other topics; it is the basis for all codes of Jewish law

Tai Shang Kan-Yin P'ien (AD twelfth-century) "Treatise of the Exalted One on Response and Retribution," covering thoughts, words, and deeds, the force field of the cosmos; it has a simple, practical approach to ethics

Quoted Authors

Aberjhani (born 1957) Born Jeffery J. Lloyd; American author, historian, columnist, novelist, poet, and editor best known as co-author of the *Encyclopedia of the Harlem Renaissance* and author of *The River of Winged Dreams*

Aristotle (384 BC–322 BC) Greek philosopher, student of Plato; scientist and tutor of Alexander the Great; wrote on various subjects: physics, biology, zoology, metaphysics, logic, ethics, aesthetics, poetry, theater, music, rhetoric, linguistics, politics and government

Stéphane Audeguy (born 1964) French, novelist and essayist
Saint Augustine (354–430) Early Christian theologian, Bishop of Hippo Regius, philosopher and saint whose writings influenced the development of Western Christianity and philosophy

William Blake (1757–1827) English poet, painter and printmaker; considered a pioneer in the arts of the Romantic Age

Niels Bohr (1885–1962) Danish physicist and philosopher who made foundational contributions to understanding atomic structure and quantum theory

Charlotte Brontë (1816–1855) English novelist and poet best known for her novel *Jane Eyre*

Sir Thomas Browne (1605–1682) English physician and author of numerous works in philosophy, science, medicine and religion

Bill Bryson (born 1951) Anglo-American author of books on travel, the English language, science and other nonfiction topics

The Buddha, also known as Siddhartha Gautama (560 BC–477 BC); Born in what is now southern Nepal, he was the son of a king; he sought and achieved enlightenment

George Gordon Byron, also known as Lord Byron (1788–1824); British poet and playwright best known for his works *Don Juan* and *Childe Harold's Pilgrimage*

Orson Scott Card (born 1951) American novelist and critic best known for science fiction work *Ender's Game*

Thomas Carlyle (1795–1881) Scottish philosopher, satirical writer, essayist, historian and teacher known for his works *On Heroes, Hero-Worship, and The Heroic in History*, *The French Revolution: A History* and *Sartor Resartus*

Carlos Castaneda (1925–1998) Peruvian-born American author, doctor of anthropology and shaman best known for his work *The Teachings of Don Juan*

Pierre Teilhard de Chardin (1881–1955) French philosopher and Jesuit priest who conceived the idea of the Omega Point, a maximum level of complexity and consciousness to which he believed the universe is evolving

Deepak Chopra (born 1947) American author, public speaker, alternative-medicine advocate and a prominent figure in the New Age movement

Paulo Coelho (born 1947) Brazilian award-winning author of *The Alchemist*

Moses ben Jacob Cordovero (1522–1570) A central figure in the development of Kabbalah and leader of a mystical school in sixteenth century Israel

Brian Cox (born 1968) English physicist and advanced fellow of particle physics in the School of Physics and Astronomy at the University of Manchester

Mihaly Csikszentmihalyi (born 1934) Hungarian psychologist and professor of psychology at Claremont Graduate University who recognized and named the psychological concept of flow, a highly focused mental state also known as the zone

Democritus (460 BC–370 BC) Ancient Greek philosopher primarily known for his formulation of an atomic theory of the universe and considered by many as the father of modern science

Albert Einstein (1879–1955) German-born physicist who developed the general theory of relativity and who is considered the most influential physicist of the twentieth century

Ralph Waldo Emerson (1803–1882) American essayist, journalist, philosopher, lecturer and poet who led the Transcendentalist movement of the mid-nineteenth century

Madeleine L'Engle (1918–2007) American author of *A Wrinkle in Time* and its sequels *A Wind in the Door*, *A Swiftly Tilting Planet*, *Many Waters* and *An Acceptable Time*

Henry Ford (1863–1947) American industrialist, founder of the Ford Motor Company, credited for developing assembly-line mass production

Benjamin Franklin (1706–1790) American author, printer, political theorist, politician, Freemason, postmaster, scientist, inventor, civic activist, statesman, diplomat and Founding Father of the United States

Robert Graves (1895–1985) English poet, novelist, critic and classicist

Brian Greene (born 1963) American theoretical physicist, string theorist, author and professor of physics and mathematics at Columbia University

Bede Griffiths (1906–1993) Born Alan Richard Griffiths and also known as Swami Dayananda "bliss of compassion"; British Benedictine monk and priest, Camaldolese monk, mystic and theologian who lived in ashrams in South India and became a yogi

Sidney J. Harris (1917–1986) London-born American author and journalist for the *Chicago Daily News* and the *Chicago Sun-Times*

Richard Conn Henry (born 1940) American author and professor of physics and astronomy at Johns Hopkins University

Hermann Hesse (1877–1962) German-born Swiss poet, novelist and painter best known for his works *Demian, Steppenwolf, Siddhartha,* and *The Glass Bead Game* in which he writes of an individual's search for truth, self-knowledge and spirituality

Bill Hicks (1961–1994) American stand-up comedian, social critic, satirist, and musician whose material, encompassed a wide range of social issues including religion, politics, and philosophy

Leonard Jacobson (born 1944) Australian spiritual teacher and author

Sir James Jeans (1877–1946) English physicist, astronomer and mathematician

Jesus Christ (4 BC–AD 29) Born in Nazareth, known as the Son of God and the founder of the Christian religion, he was crucified for his teachings

Carl Jung (1875–1961) Swiss psychiatrist, psychoanalyst and founder of analytical psychology, best known for his psychological concepts of synchronicity, archetypal phenomena and the collective unconscious

Immanuel Kant (1724–1804) German philosopher, considered the central figure of modern philosophy

Lawrence M. Krauss (born 1954) American theoretical physicist, cosmologist and author; Foundation Professor of the School of Earth and Space Exploration at Arizona State University and director of its Origins Project

Jiddu Krishnamurti (1895–1986) Indian philosopher, speaker and spiritual author

Robert Lanza (born 1956) American medical doctor, scientist and Chief Scientific Officer of Ocata Therapeutics and Adjunct Professor at the Institute for Regenerative Medicine at Wake Forest University School of Medicine

Bruce Lee (1940–1973) American actor, martial artist, philosopher, filmmaker and founder of the martial art Jeet Kune Do

Eric Micha'el Leventhal (born 1978) American author, literary consultant and holistic educator

Charles de Lint (born 1951) Dutch-born, prolific Canadian author of fantasy fiction novels, novellas, short stories and poetry

Ramana Maharshi (1879–1950) Born Venkataraman Iyer; Indian sage, guru and widely recognized enlightened being

Steve Maraboli (born 1975) American author, speaker and behavioral scientist

Jed McKenna Fictitious American author and guru who runs an ashram in Iowa

Meher Baba (1894–1969) Born Merwan Sheriar Irani, Indian spiritual master who said he was an avatar, a deity in human form

Dan Millman (born 1946) American author and lecturer in personal development best known for his book *Way of the Peaceful Warrior*

John Muir (1838–1914) Scottish-American naturalist, author, environmental philosopher, preservationist; eponym of the Muir Woods National Monument, Muir Beach, John Muir College, Mount Muir, Camp Muir and Muir Glacier

Friedrich Wilhelm Nietzsche (1844–1900) German philosopher, cultural critic, poet, philologist and scholar whose work has had a profound influence on Western philosophy

Harry Palmer (born 1944) American author and former teacher who became engaged with Scientology and later founded the Avatar Course

Plato (428BC–348 BC) Greek philosopher, founder of the Academy in Athens; considered the central figure in the development of Western philosophy

Svami Prajnanpad (1891–1974) Born Yogeshwar Chattopadhyay; Indian disciple of Niralamba Swami, the great yogi and Guru of India

Amit Ray (born 1960) Indian author and spiritual master, best known for his Om meditation, integrated yoga and Vipassana-meditation technique

Kalu Rinpoche (1905–1989) Tibetan Buddhist lama, scholar and teacher who was one of the first Tibetan masters to teach in the West

Don Miguel Ruiz (born 1952) Mexican author of Toltec spiritualist best known for his works *The Four Agreements, The Mastery Of Love, The Voice Of Knowledge* and *The Fifth Agreement*

Rumi (1207–1273) Persian thirteenth-century poet and Sufi, Islamic scholar and theologian

Carl Sagan (1934–1996) American astronomer, cosmologist, astrophysicist, astrobiologist, author and anti-nuclear activist

Sai Baba (1835–1918) Indian spiritual master regarded by his devotees as an incarnation of God, saint, fakir and satguru

Chelsie Shakespeare (born 1984) American author of the novel *The Pull*

Isaac Bashevis Singer (1902–1991) Polish-born Jewish writer best known for his works *A Day Of Pleasure: Stories of a Boy Growing Up in Warsaw* and *A Crown of Feathers and Other Stories*

John Steinbeck (1902–1968) American author best known for his works *East of Eden*, *Of Mice and Men* and *The Grapes of Wrath*

Nikola Tesla (1856–1943) Serbian American inventor, electrical engineer, mechanical engineer, physicist and futurist best known for his contributions to the design of the modern alternating-current-electricity supply system

Eckhart Tolle (born 1948) German-born Canadian resident, spiritual teacher and author best known for his books *The Power of Now* and *A New Earth: Awakening to Your Life's Purpose*

Amish Tripathi (born 1974) Indian author best known for his novels *The Immortals of Meluha*, *The Secret of the Nagas*, *The Oath of the Vayuputras* and *Scion of Ikshvaku*

Chogyam Trungpa (1939–1987) Tibetan Buddhist meditation master, teacher, poet, artist and founder of Vajradhatu and Naropa University

Neil deGrasse Tyson (born 1958) American astrophysicist, cosmologist, author and director of the Hayden Planetarium at the Rose Center for Earth and Space, in New York City

Lao Tzu (605 BC–531 BC) Chinese philosopher, writer and presumed author of the Tao Te Ching

Swami Vivekananda (1863–1902) Born Narendranath Datta; Indian Hindu monk, chief disciple of the Indian mystic Ramakrishna and a key figure in the introduction of the philosophies of Vedanta and Yoga to the Western world

Alan Watts (1915–1973) British-born American philosopher, writer, and speaker best known for interpreting and popularizing Eastern philosophy for a Western audience

Oprah Winfrey (born 1954) American media proprietor, talk-show host, actress, producer, and philanthropist best known for her talk show *The Oprah Winfrey Show*

Jeanette Winterson (born 1959) English author, professor of creative writing and journalist known for her work *Oranges Are Not the Only Fruit*

William Butler Yeats (1865–1939) Irish poet and winner of the Nobel Prize in Literature

Hamza Yusuf (born 1960) American Islamic scholar and co-founder of Zaytuna College

www.ingramcontent.com/pod-product-compliance
Lightning Source LLC
LaVergne TN
LVHW051603080426
835510LV00020B/3116